50 Ramen and Beyond Japan Dishes

By: Kelly Johnson

Table of Contents

- Tonkotsu Ramen
- Shoyu Ramen
- Miso Ramen
- Shio Ramen
- Tsukemen (Dipping Noodles)
- Hiyashi Chuka (Cold Ramen Salad)
- Ramen Burger
- Chicken Katsu Curry
- Udon Noodle Soup
- Soba Noodles with Tempura
- Yaki Udon
- Zaru Soba (Cold Soba)
- Beef Sukiyaki
- Tonkotsu Gyoza
- Okonomiyaki
- Takoyaki
- Donburi (Rice Bowl) with Beef or Chicken

- Chashu Pork Buns
- Ebi Fry (Breaded Shrimp)
- Unagi Don (Grilled Eel Rice Bowl)
- Katsu Don
- Oyakodon (Chicken and Egg Rice Bowl)
- Tamagoyaki (Japanese Omelette)
- Chirashi Sushi
- Maki Rolls (Sushi Rolls)
- Negitoro Don (Tuna and Scallion Rice Bowl)
- Omurice
- Beef Tataki
- Gyu Don (Beef Rice Bowl)
- Karaage (Japanese Fried Chicken)
- Shabu-Shabu
- Kiritanpo (Rice Stick Hot Pot)
- Yuba (Tofu Skin)
- Ebi Tempura
- Dashi Soup
- Gyoza (Dumplings)

- Tamago Sando (Egg Sandwich)
- Tofu Donburi
- Ramen Stir-Fry (Yaki Ramen)
- Mentaiko Spaghetti
- Ikayaki (Grilled Squid)
- Nikuman (Pork Bun)
- Ramen Salad
- Onigiri (Rice Balls)
- Abura Soba (Oil Noodles)
- Genovese Udon
- Nabe (Hot Pot)
- Hakata-style Motsunabe (Beef Offal Hot Pot)
- Chirashi Don (Scattered Sushi Rice Bowl)
- Mochi Ice Cream

Tonkotsu Ramen

Ingredients:

- 2 cups tonkotsu broth (pork bone broth)
- 2 servings ramen noodles
- 2 slices chashu pork
- 1 soft-boiled egg
- 1/4 cup bamboo shoots
- 2 tbsp green onions, chopped
- 1 tbsp sesame oil
- 1 tbsp soy sauce
- 1 tsp garlic paste

Instructions:

1. Prepare the ramen noodles according to the package instructions.
2. In a large bowl, pour the hot tonkotsu broth.
3. Place the cooked noodles into the broth.
4. Top with chashu pork, soft-boiled egg, bamboo shoots, and green onions.
5. Drizzle sesame oil, soy sauce, and garlic paste over the top.
6. Serve hot and enjoy!

Shoyu Ramen

Ingredients:

- 2 cups chicken or vegetable broth
- 2 tbsp soy sauce
- 2 servings ramen noodles
- 1 soft-boiled egg
- 2 slices chashu pork
- 1/4 cup nori (seaweed)
- 1/4 cup bamboo shoots
- 1 tbsp green onions, chopped
- 1 tsp sesame oil
- 1 tsp garlic paste

Instructions:

1. Prepare the ramen noodles according to the package instructions.
2. In a medium saucepan, combine chicken broth and soy sauce. Bring to a simmer.
3. Place the cooked noodles into a bowl, then pour the hot broth over the noodles.
4. Top with chashu pork, soft-boiled egg, nori, bamboo shoots, and green onions.
5. Drizzle sesame oil and garlic paste over the top.
6. Serve hot.

Miso Ramen

Ingredients:

- 2 cups chicken or vegetable broth
- 2 tbsp miso paste (red or white)
- 2 servings ramen noodles
- 2 slices chashu pork
- 1 soft-boiled egg
- 1/4 cup corn kernels
- 1/4 cup bamboo shoots
- 1 tbsp green onions, chopped
- 1 tbsp sesame oil
- 1 tsp garlic paste

Instructions:

1. Prepare the ramen noodles according to the package instructions.
2. In a medium saucepan, combine chicken broth and miso paste. Bring to a simmer, stirring until the miso dissolves.
3. Place the cooked noodles into a bowl, then pour the hot miso broth over the noodles.
4. Top with chashu pork, soft-boiled egg, corn, bamboo shoots, and green onions.
5. Drizzle sesame oil and garlic paste over the top.

6. Serve hot.

Shio Ramen

Ingredients:

- 2 cups chicken or vegetable broth
- 1 tbsp salt
- 2 servings ramen noodles
- 1 soft-boiled egg
- 2 slices chashu pork
- 1/4 cup nori (seaweed)
- 1 tbsp green onions, chopped
- 1 tsp sesame oil

Instructions:

1. Prepare the ramen noodles according to the package instructions.
2. In a medium saucepan, combine chicken broth and salt. Bring to a simmer.
3. Place the cooked noodles into a bowl, then pour the hot shio broth over the noodles.
4. Top with chashu pork, soft-boiled egg, nori, and green onions.
5. Drizzle sesame oil over the top.
6. Serve hot.

Tsukemen (Dipping Noodles)

Ingredients:

- 2 servings ramen noodles
- 2 cups chicken or pork broth
- 1 tbsp soy sauce
- 1 tbsp mirin
- 2 tbsp sesame oil
- 1/4 cup green onions, chopped
- 2 slices chashu pork
- 1 soft-boiled egg
- 1/4 cup bamboo shoots

Instructions:

1. Prepare the ramen noodles according to the package instructions. Drain and set aside.
2. In a separate bowl, combine chicken or pork broth, soy sauce, mirin, and sesame oil. Heat until warm.
3. Place the cooked noodles on a plate or in a shallow bowl.
4. Serve the dipping broth in a separate bowl alongside the noodles.
5. Garnish the noodles with chashu pork, soft-boiled egg, bamboo shoots, and green onions.
6. To eat, dip the noodles into the broth before each bite.

Hiyashi Chuka (Cold Ramen Salad)

Ingredients:

- 2 servings ramen noodles (chilled)
- 1/2 cucumber, julienned
- 1/2 carrot, julienned
- 1/4 cup cooked chicken, shredded
- 1/4 cup ham, julienned
- 2 tbsp sesame seeds
- 1/4 cup green onions, chopped
- 1 tbsp soy sauce
- 1 tbsp rice vinegar
- 1 tsp sesame oil
- 1 tsp sugar

Instructions:

1. Prepare the ramen noodles according to the package instructions, then chill them in cold water.
2. In a small bowl, whisk together soy sauce, rice vinegar, sesame oil, and sugar.
3. Arrange the chilled noodles on a plate or bowl. Top with cucumber, carrot, chicken, ham, and green onions.
4. Drizzle the dressing over the noodles and sprinkle with sesame seeds.

5. Serve cold.

Ramen Burger

Ingredients:

- 2 servings ramen noodles
- 2 beef patties (or your choice of protein)
- 2 soft-boiled eggs
- 1/4 cup lettuce
- 1/4 cup sliced tomatoes
- 2 tbsp soy sauce
- 1 tbsp sesame oil
- 1 tbsp mayonnaise
- 1 tsp Sriracha (optional)

Instructions:

1. Prepare the ramen noodles according to the package instructions. Drain and cool slightly.
2. Shape the ramen noodles into two buns by pressing them into a round mold or shaping them by hand. Fry each side in a lightly oiled pan until crispy and golden brown.
3. Cook the beef patties and assemble the burger: place the beef patty on the ramen bun, followed by a soft-boiled egg, lettuce, and tomato.
4. Mix mayonnaise and Sriracha (if using) and spread on the top ramen bun.
5. Top with the second ramen bun and serve immediately.

Chicken Katsu Curry

Ingredients:

- 2 boneless chicken breasts
- 1 cup panko breadcrumbs
- 1 egg, beaten
- 1/2 cup flour
- 2 cups curry sauce (store-bought or homemade)
- 2 cups cooked rice
- 2 tbsp vegetable oil for frying
- 1/4 cup green onions, chopped

Instructions:

1. Dredge each chicken breast in flour, dip in the beaten egg, and coat with panko breadcrumbs.
2. Heat vegetable oil in a frying pan over medium-high heat. Fry the chicken breasts until golden brown and cooked through, about 5-7 minutes per side.
3. While the chicken is frying, heat the curry sauce in a separate pot.
4. Serve the fried chicken over cooked rice and pour the hot curry sauce over the chicken.
5. Garnish with green onions and serve hot.

Udon Noodle Soup

Ingredients:

- 2 servings udon noodles
- 4 cups dashi broth (fish or vegetable stock)
- 2 tbsp soy sauce
- 1 tbsp mirin
- 2 tsp sugar
- 2 slices kamaboko (fish cake)
- 2-3 green onions, chopped
- 1 soft-boiled egg
- 1/2 cup spinach (optional)

Instructions:

1. Prepare the udon noodles according to the package instructions.
2. In a pot, combine dashi broth, soy sauce, mirin, and sugar. Bring to a simmer.
3. Add the cooked noodles to the broth and let them heat through.
4. Serve the udon noodles in a bowl, topped with kamaboko, green onions, soft-boiled egg, and spinach (optional).
5. Serve hot.

Soba Noodles with Tempura

Ingredients:

- 2 servings soba noodles
- 6-8 pieces tempura shrimp (or your choice of tempura vegetables)
- 2 tbsp soy sauce
- 1 tbsp mirin
- 1/2 cup dashi broth
- 1/4 cup green onions, chopped
- 1 tsp sesame oil
- 1 tsp grated daikon (optional)

Instructions:

1. Cook the soba noodles according to the package instructions. Drain and rinse under cold water.
2. Heat dashi broth in a pot and stir in soy sauce and mirin.
3. Serve the soba noodles in a bowl and pour the warm broth over the noodles.
4. Arrange tempura shrimp or vegetables on top.
5. Garnish with green onions, sesame oil, and grated daikon.
6. Serve immediately.

Yaki Udon

Ingredients:

- 2 servings udon noodles
- 1/2 cup sliced shiitake mushrooms
- 1/2 cup sliced bell peppers
- 1/4 cup sliced carrots
- 2 tbsp soy sauce
- 1 tbsp oyster sauce
- 1 tbsp mirin
- 1 tbsp vegetable oil
- 1/2 cup cooked chicken or beef (optional)
- 2 green onions, chopped

Instructions:

1. Cook the udon noodles according to the package instructions. Drain and set aside.
2. Heat vegetable oil in a pan over medium-high heat and sauté the mushrooms, bell peppers, and carrots until tender.
3. Add the cooked noodles, soy sauce, oyster sauce, and mirin. Toss to coat and cook for 2-3 minutes.
4. Add cooked chicken or beef if desired.
5. Garnish with green onions and serve hot.

Zaru Soba (Cold Soba)

Ingredients:

- 2 servings soba noodles
- 1/4 cup soy sauce
- 1/4 cup mirin
- 1/4 cup dashi broth
- 1 tbsp sugar
- 1 tsp wasabi (optional)
- 2 tbsp green onions, chopped
- 1 tbsp sesame seeds (optional)

Instructions:

1. Cook the soba noodles according to the package instructions. Drain and rinse under cold water.
2. In a small bowl, mix soy sauce, mirin, dashi broth, and sugar to make the dipping sauce.
3. Serve the cold soba noodles on a plate with a side of dipping sauce.
4. Garnish with green onions, sesame seeds, and wasabi if desired.
5. To eat, dip the soba noodles into the sauce before each bite.

Beef Sukiyaki

Ingredients:

- 1/2 lb thinly sliced beef (ribeye or sirloin)
- 2 cups dashi broth
- 3 tbsp soy sauce
- 2 tbsp mirin
- 2 tbsp sugar
- 1/2 cup shiitake mushrooms, sliced
- 1/2 cup napa cabbage, chopped
- 1/2 cup tofu, cubed
- 2 green onions, chopped
- 2 soft-boiled eggs (optional)

Instructions:

1. In a large skillet or hot pot, heat dashi broth, soy sauce, mirin, and sugar over medium heat.
2. Add the beef slices to the broth and cook until just browned.
3. Add the mushrooms, cabbage, tofu, and green onions. Simmer for 5-7 minutes until the vegetables are tender.
4. Serve the sukiyaki hot with soft-boiled eggs on the side if desired.
5. Enjoy the dish by dipping the beef and vegetables into the broth.

Tonkotsu Gyoza

Ingredients:

- 1/2 lb ground pork
- 1/4 cup chopped cabbage
- 2 tbsp chopped green onions
- 2 tbsp soy sauce
- 1 tsp ginger, minced
- 1 tsp garlic, minced
- 20 gyoza wrappers
- 1 tbsp vegetable oil
- 1 tbsp sesame oil
- Soy sauce for dipping

Instructions:

1. In a bowl, combine the ground pork, cabbage, green onions, soy sauce, ginger, and garlic. Mix until well combined.
2. Place a small spoonful of the filling in the center of each gyoza wrapper.
3. Wet the edges of the wrapper and fold to form a half-moon shape, pinching the edges to seal.
4. Heat vegetable oil and sesame oil in a pan over medium heat. Fry the gyoza for 2-3 minutes until the bottoms are golden brown.

5. Add 1/4 cup of water to the pan and cover. Steam for another 5 minutes until the gyoza are cooked through.

6. Serve with soy sauce for dipping.

Okonomiyaki

Ingredients:

- 1 cup flour
- 1/2 cup dashi broth
- 1 egg
- 1/4 head cabbage, shredded
- 2 green onions, chopped
- 1/4 cup cooked bacon or pork belly (optional)
- 2 tbsp soy sauce
- 2 tbsp mayonnaise
- 2 tbsp okonomiyaki sauce (or Worcestershire sauce)

Instructions:

1. In a large bowl, mix the flour, dashi broth, egg, cabbage, and green onions.
2. Heat a pan over medium heat and add a little oil.
3. Pour the batter into the pan, shaping it into a round pancake. Cook for 3-4 minutes on each side until golden brown.
4. Drizzle soy sauce, mayonnaise, and okonomiyaki sauce on top.
5. Serve immediately.

Takoyaki

Ingredients:

- 1 cup takoyaki flour (or all-purpose flour with a pinch of dashi powder)
- 1 1/2 cups water
- 1 egg
- 1/4 cup pickled ginger, chopped
- 1/4 lb octopus, cooked and chopped
- 2 tbsp green onions, chopped
- 2 tbsp soy sauce
- 2 tbsp takoyaki sauce (or Worcestershire sauce)
- 2 tbsp bonito flakes (optional)

Instructions:

1. In a bowl, whisk together the takoyaki flour, water, and egg until smooth.
2. Heat a takoyaki pan and brush with oil.
3. Pour the batter into the molds and add octopus, pickled ginger, and green onions into each one.
4. Cook for 3-4 minutes, turning the takoyaki balls with chopsticks to cook evenly.
5. Drizzle takoyaki sauce on top and sprinkle with bonito flakes.
6. Serve hot.

Donburi (Rice Bowl) with Beef or Chicken

Ingredients:

- 2 cups cooked rice
- 1/2 lb beef or chicken, thinly sliced
- 1/4 cup soy sauce
- 2 tbsp mirin
- 1 tbsp sugar
- 1/4 cup green onions, chopped
- 1 soft-boiled egg (optional)

Instructions:

1. In a skillet, combine soy sauce, mirin, and sugar. Add the beef or chicken slices and cook until the meat is fully cooked and the sauce thickens.
2. Serve the cooked meat over a bowl of rice.
3. Top with green onions and a soft-boiled egg if desired.
4. Serve immediately.

Chashu Pork Buns

Ingredients:

- 1/2 lb chashu pork (or braised pork belly)
- 12 steamed bao buns (store-bought or homemade)
- 2 tbsp soy sauce
- 1 tbsp hoisin sauce
- 1 tbsp green onions, chopped

Instructions:

1. Slice the chashu pork into thin pieces.
2. Heat the bao buns in a steamer or microwave.
3. Fill each bao bun with chashu pork, drizzle with soy sauce and hoisin sauce, and garnish with green onions.
4. Serve immediately.

Ebi Fry (Breaded Shrimp)

Ingredients:

- 10 large shrimp, peeled and deveined
- 1/2 cup flour
- 1 egg, beaten
- 1 cup panko breadcrumbs
- Vegetable oil for frying
- Tartar sauce for dipping

Instructions:

1. Dredge each shrimp in flour, dip into the beaten egg, and coat with panko breadcrumbs.
2. Heat vegetable oil in a pan over medium heat.
3. Fry the shrimp for 3-4 minutes until golden and crispy.
4. Serve with tartar sauce for dipping.

Unagi Don (Grilled Eel Rice Bowl)

Ingredients:

- 2 servings grilled eel (unagi), sliced
- 2 cups cooked white rice
- 1/4 cup unagi sauce (or eel sauce)
- 1 tbsp sesame seeds
- 2 tbsp pickled ginger (optional)
- 1/4 cup green onions, chopped

Instructions:

1. Prepare the grilled eel according to package instructions (or grill fresh eel if available).
2. Serve the cooked rice in bowls, placing slices of eel on top.
3. Drizzle unagi sauce over the eel and rice.
4. Garnish with sesame seeds, pickled ginger, and green onions.
5. Serve immediately.

Katsu Don

Ingredients:

- 1 serving breaded and fried pork cutlet (tonkatsu)
- 2 cups cooked rice
- 1/4 cup onions, sliced
- 2 eggs, beaten
- 2 tbsp soy sauce
- 2 tbsp mirin
- 1 tbsp sugar
- 1/4 cup dashi broth

Instructions:

1. Prepare the tonkatsu (breaded and fried pork cutlet) and slice into strips.
2. In a pan, combine soy sauce, mirin, sugar, and dashi broth. Bring to a simmer.
3. Add the sliced onions and cook until softened.
4. Pour the beaten eggs over the onions and simmer until the eggs are partially set.
5. Place the sliced tonkatsu over the eggs, cover, and let cook for 2-3 minutes until fully set.
6. Serve over a bowl of cooked rice.

Oyakodon (Chicken and Egg Rice Bowl)

Ingredients:

- 2 chicken thighs, boneless and skinless, cut into bite-sized pieces
- 2 eggs, beaten
- 2 cups cooked rice
- 1/4 cup onions, sliced
- 2 tbsp soy sauce
- 2 tbsp mirin
- 1 tbsp sugar
- 1/4 cup dashi broth
- 1 tbsp green onions, chopped

Instructions:

1. In a skillet, combine soy sauce, mirin, sugar, and dashi broth. Bring to a simmer.
2. Add the chicken pieces and cook until the chicken is no longer pink.
3. Add the sliced onions and cook until soft.
4. Pour the beaten eggs over the chicken and onions, cover, and cook until the eggs are set.
5. Serve over a bowl of cooked rice.
6. Garnish with chopped green onions.

Tamagoyaki (Japanese Omelette)

Ingredients:

- 4 eggs
- 1 tbsp soy sauce
- 1 tbsp mirin
- 1 tsp sugar
- 1 tbsp vegetable oil

Instructions:

1. In a bowl, whisk together the eggs, soy sauce, mirin, and sugar.
2. Heat a tamagoyaki pan (or non-stick skillet) over medium heat and lightly oil it.
3. Pour a thin layer of the egg mixture into the pan, swirling to cover the bottom.
4. Once the egg sets, roll it up into a log. Push the roll to the back of the pan.
5. Pour more egg mixture into the pan, lifting the roll to allow the egg to flow underneath.
6. Roll up the new layer over the existing roll and repeat until all the eggs are used.
7. Slice the tamagoyaki into bite-sized pieces and serve.

Chirashi Sushi

Ingredients:

- 2 cups sushi rice, cooked and seasoned with rice vinegar, sugar, and salt
- 1/2 lb assorted sashimi-grade fish (tuna, salmon, etc.), sliced
- 1/4 cup cucumber, julienned
- 1/4 cup avocado, sliced
- 1/4 cup pickled ginger
- 1 tbsp sesame seeds
- 1 tbsp nori (seaweed) strips
- 1 tbsp wasabi (optional)

Instructions:

1. Prepare sushi rice and let it cool slightly.
2. Spoon the rice into bowls and top with slices of sashimi-grade fish.
3. Arrange cucumber, avocado, pickled ginger, and nori on top.
4. Sprinkle with sesame seeds and serve with wasabi on the side if desired.

Maki Rolls (Sushi Rolls)

Ingredients:

- 2 cups sushi rice, cooked and seasoned with rice vinegar, sugar, and salt
- 1 sheet nori (seaweed)
- 1/2 cucumber, julienned
- 1/2 avocado, sliced
- 1/4 lb sashimi-grade fish (tuna, salmon, etc.), sliced
- Soy sauce for dipping
- Wasabi and pickled ginger (optional)

Instructions:

1. Place a sheet of nori on a bamboo sushi mat.
2. Spread a thin layer of sushi rice evenly over the nori, leaving a 1-inch border at the top.
3. Arrange cucumber, avocado, and sashimi-grade fish in the center.
4. Roll the sushi tightly using the sushi mat, sealing the edge with a little water.
5. Slice the roll into bite-sized pieces and serve with soy sauce, wasabi, and pickled ginger.

Negitoro Don (Tuna and Scallion Rice Bowl)

Ingredients:

- 1/2 lb fresh tuna, minced
- 1/4 cup scallions, chopped
- 1 tbsp soy sauce
- 1 tsp sesame oil
- 2 cups cooked rice
- 1 tbsp sesame seeds
- 1 tbsp nori strips

Instructions:

1. In a bowl, mix the minced tuna with soy sauce, sesame oil, and scallions.
2. Serve the mixture over a bowl of cooked rice.
3. Garnish with sesame seeds and nori strips.
4. Serve immediately.

Omurice

Ingredients:

- 2 cups cooked rice
- 1/4 cup onions, diced
- 1/4 cup cooked chicken, diced (optional)
- 1/4 cup ketchup
- 2 eggs, beaten
- 1 tbsp vegetable oil
- 1 tbsp soy sauce (optional)
- Salt and pepper to taste

Instructions:

1. In a skillet, heat vegetable oil and sauté onions until soft.
2. Add the cooked rice and chicken, then stir in ketchup and soy sauce. Cook until heated through.
3. In a separate pan, make a thin omelette by cooking the beaten eggs over medium heat.
4. Spoon the rice mixture into the center of the omelette, then fold the edges over to cover the rice.
5. Serve hot, garnished with additional ketchup if desired.

Beef Tataki

Ingredients:

- 1/2 lb beef tenderloin
- 2 tbsp soy sauce
- 1 tbsp mirin
- 1 tbsp rice vinegar
- 1 tsp sesame oil
- 1/4 cup green onions, chopped
- 1 tbsp sesame seeds

Instructions:

1. Sear the beef in a hot pan for 1-2 minutes on each side, then remove and let cool.
2. Slice the beef thinly and arrange on a plate.
3. Mix soy sauce, mirin, rice vinegar, and sesame oil in a bowl.
4. Drizzle the sauce over the sliced beef.
5. Garnish with green onions and sesame seeds, and serve.

Gyu Don (Beef Rice Bowl)

Ingredients:

- 1/2 lb thinly sliced beef (ribeye or sirloin)
- 2 cups cooked rice
- 1/4 cup onions, sliced
- 2 tbsp soy sauce
- 2 tbsp mirin
- 1 tbsp sugar
- 1/4 cup dashi broth
- 1 soft-boiled egg (optional)
- 1 tbsp green onions, chopped

Instructions:

1. In a pan, combine soy sauce, mirin, sugar, and dashi broth. Bring to a simmer.
2. Add the sliced beef and cook until browned.
3. Add the onions and cook until tender.
4. Serve the beef mixture over a bowl of rice.
5. Top with a soft-boiled egg and garnish with green onions.

Karaage (Japanese Fried Chicken)

Ingredients:

- 1 lb chicken thighs, cut into bite-sized pieces
- 2 tbsp soy sauce
- 1 tbsp sake
- 1 tbsp grated ginger
- 1 tbsp garlic, minced
- 1 tbsp sugar
- 1/2 cup cornstarch
- Vegetable oil for frying
- Lemon wedges (for serving)

Instructions:

1. In a bowl, mix soy sauce, sake, ginger, garlic, and sugar. Add the chicken pieces and marinate for 30 minutes.
2. Heat oil in a deep pan or fryer to 350°F (175°C).
3. Coat the marinated chicken in cornstarch, pressing lightly to ensure an even coat.
4. Fry the chicken pieces in batches until golden brown and crispy, about 5-7 minutes.
5. Drain on paper towels and serve with lemon wedges.

Shabu-Shabu

Ingredients:

- 1 lb thinly sliced beef (or pork)
- 6 cups dashi broth (or water with kombu and bonito flakes)
- 1/2 cup soy sauce
- 1/4 cup mirin
- 1 tbsp sesame oil
- 1 cup napa cabbage, chopped
- 1 cup shiitake mushrooms, sliced
- 1/2 cup tofu, cubed
- 1/2 cup udon noodles (optional)
- Dipping sauce (ponzu sauce and sesame sauce)

Instructions:

1. Bring the dashi broth to a boil in a hot pot or large saucepan.
2. Add soy sauce, mirin, and sesame oil to the broth and simmer.
3. Add vegetables, tofu, and mushrooms to the broth and cook for 2-3 minutes.
4. Add the thinly sliced beef or pork to the hot broth and cook for about 30 seconds to 1 minute.
5. Serve with ponzu sauce and sesame sauce for dipping, and optional cooked udon noodles.

Kiritanpo (Rice Stick Hot Pot)

Ingredients:

- 2 cups cooked rice
- 1 tbsp soy sauce
- 1 tsp salt
- 1/4 cup mirin
- 1/4 cup sake
- 1 lb chicken thighs, boneless, and skinless
- 1 cup shiitake mushrooms, sliced
- 1/2 cup napa cabbage, chopped
- 2 tbsp sesame oil
- 4 cups dashi broth

Instructions:

1. Mash the cooked rice with soy sauce and salt, then form the rice into long cylindrical shapes (sticks).
2. Grill the rice sticks on a medium heat until slightly browned and crispy, then set aside.
3. In a hot pot, heat the dashi broth and add mirin, sake, and chicken thighs. Cook the chicken for 10 minutes.
4. Add the mushrooms, cabbage, and rice sticks to the pot and cook until tender, about 5-7 minutes.

5. Serve in individual bowls and enjoy!

Yuba (Tofu Skin)

Ingredients:

- 1 block fresh tofu
- 1 cup water
- 1 tbsp soy sauce
- 1 tsp sesame oil
- 1 tbsp rice vinegar
- 1 tsp sugar

Instructions:

1. Bring the water to a simmer in a small pot and add the tofu. Simmer for 10 minutes until tofu becomes soft.
2. Remove the tofu from the water and place a cloth over the surface to collect the tofu skin (yuba).
3. Gently lift the tofu skin from the surface of the water and set it aside.
4. Mix soy sauce, sesame oil, rice vinegar, and sugar to create a dipping sauce.
5. Serve the yuba with the dipping sauce.

Ebi Tempura

Ingredients:

- 10 large shrimp, peeled and deveined
- 1/2 cup all-purpose flour
- 1/4 cup cornstarch
- 1/4 tsp baking powder
- 1/4 cup cold sparkling water
- Vegetable oil for frying
- Salt for seasoning

Instructions:

1. Prepare the batter by mixing flour, cornstarch, baking powder, and sparkling water until smooth.
2. Heat oil in a deep pan or fryer to 350°F (175°C).
3. Dip the shrimp into the batter, coating evenly, and fry until golden brown, about 2-3 minutes.
4. Drain on paper towels and season with salt. Serve with tempura dipping sauce.

Dashi Soup

Ingredients:

- 4 cups water
- 1 piece kombu (dried seaweed)
- 1/4 cup bonito flakes (dried fish flakes)
- 1 tbsp soy sauce
- 1 tbsp mirin

Instructions:

1. In a pot, bring the water and kombu to a boil, then remove the kombu.
2. Add the bonito flakes and simmer for about 5 minutes, then strain the broth to remove the flakes.
3. Add soy sauce and mirin to the broth and simmer for another 2 minutes.
4. Serve hot as a light soup base or dipping sauce.

Gyoza (Dumplings)

Ingredients:

- 1/2 lb ground pork
- 1/2 cup napa cabbage, finely chopped
- 1/4 cup green onions, chopped
- 1 tbsp soy sauce
- 1 tsp sesame oil
- 1/2 tsp garlic, minced
- 1 package gyoza wrappers
- Vegetable oil for frying

Instructions:

1. Mix the ground pork, cabbage, green onions, soy sauce, sesame oil, and garlic in a bowl.
2. Place a spoonful of filling onto each gyoza wrapper and fold to form a crescent shape, sealing the edges with water.
3. Heat oil in a pan and fry the gyoza until crispy, about 3-4 minutes.
4. Add a small amount of water to the pan, cover, and steam for another 3-4 minutes until cooked through.
5. Serve with dipping sauce (soy sauce, vinegar, and chili oil).

Tamago Sando (Egg Sandwich)

Ingredients:

- 4 slices of soft white bread
- 3 hard-boiled eggs, chopped
- 2 tbsp mayonnaise
- 1 tsp Dijon mustard
- Salt and pepper to taste

Instructions:

1. In a bowl, combine chopped hard-boiled eggs, mayonnaise, mustard, salt, and pepper.
2. Spread the egg mixture onto two slices of bread.
3. Top with the remaining slices of bread to form sandwiches.
4. Slice into halves and serve.

Tofu Donburi

Ingredients:

- 2 cups cooked rice
- 1 block tofu, pressed and cubed
- 2 tbsp soy sauce
- 1 tbsp mirin
- 1 tbsp sesame oil
- 1/4 cup green onions, chopped
- 1 tbsp sesame seeds

Instructions:

1. In a pan, heat sesame oil and sauté the tofu cubes until golden brown.
2. Add soy sauce and mirin to the tofu, cooking for another 2 minutes to coat the tofu.
3. Serve the tofu mixture over a bowl of cooked rice.
4. Garnish with green onions and sesame seeds.

Ramen Stir-Fry (Yaki Ramen)

Ingredients:

- 2 servings cooked ramen noodles
- 1/2 cup chicken breast, thinly sliced
- 1/4 cup carrots, julienned
- 1/4 cup bell peppers, sliced
- 2 tbsp soy sauce
- 1 tbsp sesame oil
- 1 tbsp mirin
- 1 tbsp sesame seeds

Instructions:

1. In a pan, heat sesame oil and sauté the chicken slices until cooked through.
2. Add the carrots and bell peppers, cooking until tender.
3. Add the cooked ramen noodles to the pan, tossing with soy sauce and mirin.
4. Stir-fry the mixture for 2-3 minutes, then serve garnished with sesame seeds.

Mentaiko Spaghetti

Ingredients:

- 8 oz spaghetti
- 1/2 cup mentaiko (cod roe), removed from the sacs
- 1/4 cup heavy cream
- 2 tbsp unsalted butter
- 1 tbsp soy sauce
- 1 tbsp sake
- 1/4 cup green onions, chopped
- Seaweed flakes for garnish (optional)

Instructions:

1. Cook the spaghetti in salted water according to the package instructions until al dente. Drain and set aside, reserving some pasta water.
2. In a pan, melt the butter and sauté the mentaiko for 1-2 minutes on medium heat.
3. Add the soy sauce and sake, stirring to combine.
4. Pour in the heavy cream and cook for an additional 2 minutes, adjusting the sauce's consistency with reserved pasta water if necessary.
5. Add the cooked spaghetti to the pan, tossing to coat the noodles in the sauce.
6. Garnish with green onions and seaweed flakes. Serve immediately.

Ikayaki (Grilled Squid)

Ingredients:

- 1 whole squid, cleaned and gutted
- 2 tbsp soy sauce
- 1 tbsp sake
- 1 tbsp mirin
- 1 tbsp sugar
- 1 tsp grated ginger
- 1 tbsp vegetable oil
- Lemon wedges for serving

Instructions:

1. In a small bowl, mix soy sauce, sake, mirin, sugar, and grated ginger to make the marinade.
2. Score the squid lightly in a crisscross pattern on both sides.
3. Marinate the squid in the sauce for at least 20 minutes.
4. Heat a grill or grill pan over medium heat and brush with vegetable oil.
5. Grill the squid for about 3-4 minutes per side, brushing with the marinade as it cooks.
6. Once grilled, slice the squid into rings and serve with lemon wedges.

Nikuman (Pork Bun)

Ingredients:

- 1 lb ground pork
- 1/4 cup onion, finely chopped
- 2 tbsp soy sauce
- 1 tbsp oyster sauce
- 1 tbsp sugar
- 1/2 tsp ground white pepper
- 1/2 tsp grated ginger
- 1 tbsp sesame oil
- 10-12 bao buns (store-bought or homemade)

Instructions:

1. In a bowl, combine the ground pork, chopped onion, soy sauce, oyster sauce, sugar, white pepper, ginger, and sesame oil. Mix well.
2. Steam the bao buns according to package instructions (or steam homemade buns).
3. Once the buns are ready, stuff each bun with the pork mixture, folding the dough over the filling to seal.
4. Steam the filled buns for 15-20 minutes until the pork is cooked through and the buns are soft and fluffy.
5. Serve hot.

Ramen Salad

Ingredients:

- 1 package instant ramen noodles (discard seasoning packet)
- 1/2 cup shredded cabbage
- 1/4 cup shredded carrots
- 1/4 cup green onions, chopped
- 1/4 cup sliced cucumber
- 1/4 cup roasted peanuts (optional)

Dressing:

- 3 tbsp soy sauce
- 1 tbsp rice vinegar
- 1 tbsp sesame oil
- 1 tbsp sugar
- 1 tsp grated ginger
- 1 tsp sesame seeds

Instructions:

1. Cook the ramen noodles according to package instructions, then rinse with cold water to cool. Drain well.
2. In a large bowl, combine the noodles, shredded cabbage, carrots, green onions, and cucumber.

3. In a small bowl, whisk together the soy sauce, rice vinegar, sesame oil, sugar, grated ginger, and sesame seeds for the dressing.

4. Pour the dressing over the noodles and toss to combine.

5. Garnish with roasted peanuts (optional) and serve chilled.

Onigiri (Rice Balls)

Ingredients:

- 2 cups cooked Japanese short-grain rice (sushi rice)
- 1 tbsp rice vinegar
- 1 tsp sugar
- 1/4 tsp salt
- 2-3 sheets nori (seaweed), cut into strips
- 1/2 cup filling of your choice (tuna, umeboshi, salmon, or pickled vegetables)
- Water (for moistening hands)

Instructions:

1. Mix rice vinegar, sugar, and salt in a small bowl until dissolved.
2. Add the vinegar mixture to the cooked rice, stirring gently to season the rice. Allow it to cool slightly.
3. Wet your hands with water to prevent sticking. Take a small handful of rice and flatten it in your palm.
4. Place a spoonful of filling in the center of the rice, then mold the rice around the filling into a triangle or oval shape.
5. Wrap the rice ball with a strip of nori on one side and serve.

Abura Soba (Oil Noodles)

Ingredients:

- 8 oz ramen noodles (fresh or dried)
- 2 tbsp sesame oil
- 1 tbsp soy sauce
- 1 tbsp rice vinegar
- 1 tsp sugar
- 1 tsp chili oil (optional)
- 1/4 cup chopped green onions
- 1 boiled egg, halved
- 1 tbsp toasted sesame seeds
- Nori (seaweed) strips for garnish

Instructions:

1. Cook the ramen noodles according to package instructions. Drain and rinse under cold water to cool.
2. In a small bowl, mix together the sesame oil, soy sauce, rice vinegar, sugar, and chili oil (if using).
3. Toss the cooked noodles in the sauce until well-coated.
4. Top with the boiled egg halves, chopped green onions, sesame seeds, and nori strips.
5. Serve chilled or at room temperature.

Genovese Udon

Ingredients:

- 8 oz udon noodles
- 1/4 cup olive oil
- 2 tbsp garlic, minced
- 1 cup fresh basil leaves
- 1/4 cup Parmesan cheese, grated
- 1 tbsp pine nuts (optional)
- Salt and pepper to taste

Instructions:

1. Cook the udon noodles according to package instructions, then drain and set aside.
2. In a large pan, heat the olive oil over medium heat. Add the minced garlic and cook for 1-2 minutes until fragrant.
3. Add the fresh basil and cook for another 2 minutes until the basil begins to wilt.
4. Toss the cooked udon noodles into the pan, stirring to coat the noodles in the basil and garlic oil.
5. Remove from heat and stir in the grated Parmesan cheese. Season with salt and pepper to taste.
6. Garnish with pine nuts (optional) and serve.

Nabe (Hot Pot)

Ingredients:

- 4 cups dashi broth (or chicken broth)
- 1/2 lb thinly sliced beef or pork
- 1/2 lb tofu, cut into cubes
- 1/2 head napa cabbage, chopped
- 1/2 cup shiitake mushrooms, sliced
- 1/2 cup enoki mushrooms, trimmed
- 1 medium carrot, thinly sliced
- 2-3 green onions, chopped
- 1/4 cup soy sauce
- 1 tbsp mirin
- 1 tbsp sake
- 1 tbsp sesame oil

Instructions:

1. In a large pot, bring the dashi broth to a simmer over medium heat.
2. Add the soy sauce, mirin, sake, and sesame oil to the broth, stirring to combine.
3. Add the beef or pork, tofu, napa cabbage, mushrooms, carrot, and green onions into the pot. Let the ingredients cook for 10-15 minutes, or until tender.

4. Serve the hot pot directly from the pot, allowing diners to scoop out their desired portions of meat, vegetables, and broth.

Hakata-style Motsunabe (Beef Offal Hot Pot)

Ingredients:

- 1 lb beef offal (tripe, intestines, or other parts), cleaned and cut into bite-sized pieces
- 4 cups beef broth
- 1/2 onion, sliced
- 2 tbsp soy sauce
- 1 tbsp miso paste
- 1 tbsp sake
- 2 garlic cloves, minced
- 1-inch piece of ginger, sliced
- 1/2 lb napa cabbage, chopped
- 1/4 cup chopped green onions
- 1/2 cup tofu, cut into cubes

Instructions:

1. In a large pot, combine the beef broth, soy sauce, miso paste, sake, garlic, and ginger. Bring to a simmer.

2. Add the beef offal pieces to the pot and cook for 10-15 minutes until tender.

3. Add the sliced onion, napa cabbage, and tofu cubes to the pot. Simmer for an additional 5-10 minutes until the vegetables are cooked through.

4. Garnish with chopped green onions and serve the hot pot with rice or dipping sauce.

Chirashi Don (Scattered Sushi Rice Bowl)

Ingredients:

- 2 cups sushi rice, cooked and seasoned with rice vinegar, sugar, and salt
- 1/2 lb sashimi-grade tuna, sliced
- 1/2 lb sashimi-grade salmon, sliced
- 1/4 cup cucumber, thinly sliced
- 1/4 cup pickled ginger
- 1/4 cup avocado, sliced
- 1 tbsp sesame seeds
- 1 tbsp soy sauce
- 1 tsp wasabi (optional)

Instructions:

1. Place the seasoned sushi rice into a bowl and spread it out evenly.
2. Arrange the tuna, salmon, cucumber, pickled ginger, and avocado on top of the rice.
3. Sprinkle with sesame seeds and drizzle with soy sauce. Add wasabi if desired.
4. Serve immediately as a refreshing and flavorful rice bowl.

Mochi Ice Cream

Ingredients:

- 2 cups sweet rice flour (mochi flour)
- 1/2 cup sugar
- 1 cup water
- 1/4 tsp salt
- 1 pint ice cream (flavor of your choice, such as vanilla, matcha, or red bean)
- Cornstarch for dusting

Instructions:

1. In a mixing bowl, combine the sweet rice flour, sugar, and salt.
2. Slowly add the water and stir until the mixture forms a smooth batter.
3. Pour the batter into a heatproof dish and steam over medium heat for 20-25 minutes, or until the mixture thickens and becomes translucent.
4. Once cooked, let the mochi dough cool slightly, then dust a clean surface with cornstarch.
5. Roll the dough into a thin sheet, then cut into small squares large enough to wrap around a small ball of ice cream.
6. Take small scoops of ice cream and wrap the mochi dough around them, sealing the edges.
7. Place the mochi ice cream balls on a tray and freeze for at least 2 hours before serving.